SEIZE THE A:

CRIMINAL JUSTICE WORD-PAIRS

DIFFERING BY A SINGLE CHARACTER

Wayne L. Davis, Ph.D.

SEIZE THE A:
CRIMINAL JUSTICE WORD-PAIRS DIFFERING BY A SINGLE CHARACTER

BEAT
BET

PRESENTED ARE WORD-PAIRS SUCH THAT THE SECOND WORD WOULD BE IDENTICAL
TO THE FIRST WORD IF ONE CHARACTER HAD NOT BEEN SEIZED AND REMOVED.

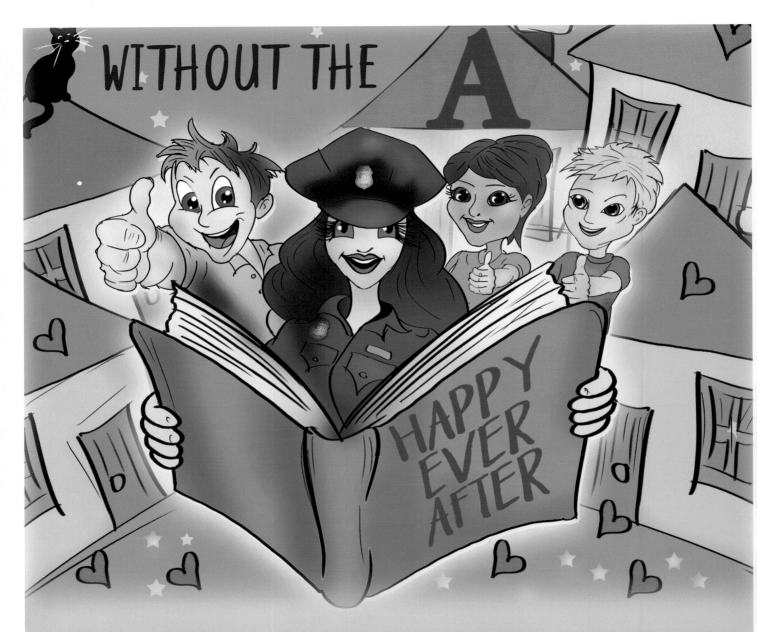

Police officers who get **ALONG** with local residents will develop **LONG** lasting relationships.

WITHOUT THE

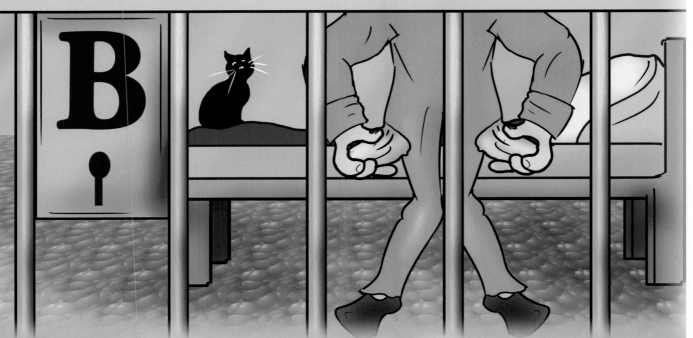

B

If defendants fail to make **BAIL**, then they will experience the **AIL** of waiting in jail.

WITHOUT A

D

QUOTAS

Residents may **DREAD** what they have **READ** about police department quotas.

Private detectives may monitor a **SITE**, which may require them to **SIT** for hours at a time.

Officers will GLISTEN if they learn to LISTEN.

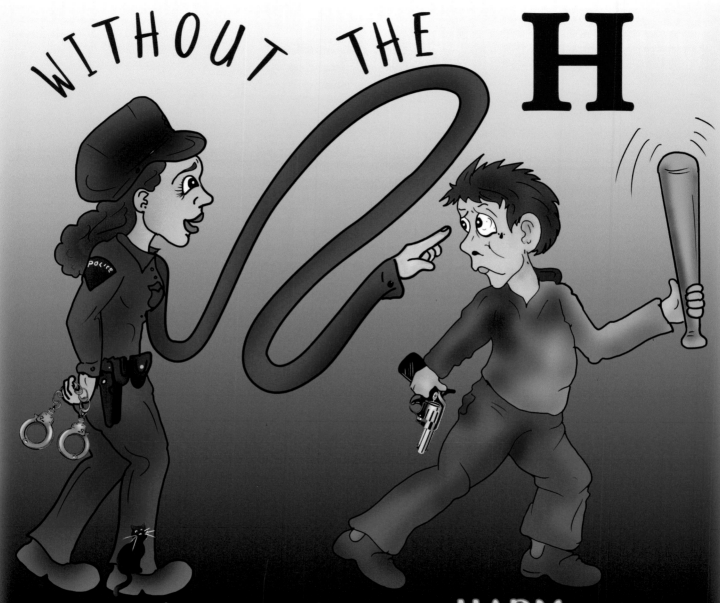

The chief will put **HEAT** on officers who **EAT** food for free.

WITHOUT THE **I**

When a police officer becomes **IRATE**, the public will **RATE** the legality of the officer's actions.

The KNAVE was arrested at the NAVE.

WITHOUT THE **L**

The animal control officer climbed the **LADDER** to avoid the **ADDER**.

An intoxicated person may **MUTTER** statements that are **UTTER** nonsense.

WITHOUT THE

N

Stay on your own **LAWN,**
as required by **LAW.**

POLICE REPORT
Dropped a Dime
SWAG
Alley Apple
Ride the Lightning
3 Hots and a Cot

WITHOUT THE N

A police report written in SLANG is worth its weight in SLAG.

WITHOUT THE **O**

Individuals who offer others the **OLIVE** branch may **LIVE** in peace.

WITHOUT THE O

LEVEL

LEVEL

LEVEL

LEVEL

Risk

Alert level **ORANGE** is high risk and has a **RANGE** of recommended protective actions.

WITHOUT THE **R**

In the **COUNTRY** is the **COUNTY**.

WITHOUT THE S

The police **SQUAD** trained in the **QUAD**.

WITHOUT THE T

Before an officer **TANGLES**,
the officer must learn the **ANGLES**.

WITHOUT THE **U**

To combat a **HOUSE** fire,
a public safety officer will use a fire **HOSE**.

WITHOUT THE W

YES NO MAYBE

WOMEN serving as public decision-makers represent a good OMEN for change.

WITHOUT THE

X

The detectives are looking for the **NEXT** mobsters for which to drag the **NET**.

WITHOUT THE

Y

During civil forfeiture, the police will say,
"What is **YOURS** is **OURS**."

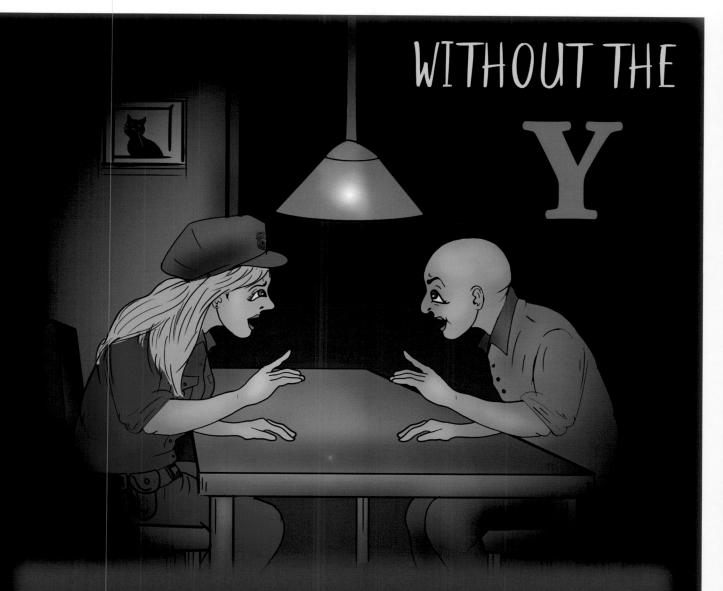

Author
Wayne L. Davis, Ph.D.

Wayne L. Davis has an electrical engineering,
business, and law enforcement
background. He has over 20 years of law
enforcement experience with city,
state, and federal law enforcement agencies.

Illustrator
Dawn Larder, Ba (Hons).

Dawn Larder is an artist and designer
specialising in book illustration.
She has illustrated for authors worldwide
across a variety of genres. Similarly, she loves
to read books of all genres, but has a
particular interest in criminology.

Printed in the United States
By Bookmasters